# Shaking the Trees
by Azra Tabassum

**WORDS DANCE PUBLISHING**
WordsDance.com

1st Edition
ISBN-13: 978-0692232408
ISBN-10: 0692232400

Editing & proofread by Amanda Oaks
Cover & interior design by Amanda Oaks

**Words Dance Publishing**
WordsDance.com

*For dada, even now, you're the strongest woman
I ever did know. I was lucky to be
your granddaughter.*

*And my parents, you don't know about this
but I hope you're proud.*

# Shaking the Trees
## AZRA TABASSUM

# Shaking the Trees

# January

We meet for the first time outside of the local Co-Op and there is nothing special about this night. It is not fog nor sleet, I am not soaked to the bone and you are not brooding quietly cigarette in hand. Instead I can't quite feel my fingers, the English cold bites down at my bones and you're sitting on a bench breathing heavily into a paper bag.

I ask if you're alright.

You snarl, "Fuck off," without looking up.

I should leave but I can't, there's something sad about a boy who can't breathe properly. There's something mournful about lungs that don't work.

I sit beside you at least two feet away and you swear a blue streak so wide that even my father would blush.

"Are you still here?" You ask through several deep breaths.

"Yes," I say. "Do you want me to call someone for you?"

"I want you to leave me the hell alone."

"But if you die here I'm sure I'll be responsible somehow."

You take a deep, rattling breath that is somehow colder than the winter and shake out the words, "I hereby allay you of all responsibility with regards to my foreseeable and impending doom."

"Wow," I say. "Funny, even on the brink of ruin, how do you do it?"

"I'm inherently optimistic. Leave me alone."

"No."

I sit with you for the next forty minutes until your breathing has evened out distinctly, and then I leave quietly. I do not ask, nor want your name.

# THIS IS HOW YOU WILL FALL IN LOVE

*Shit.*

It will happen like this: there is no thunder or roar. The weather does not change for you, there is no storm. You will not realise that the sky is softly breathing into the back of your neck. You will not realise that it is telling you to put your armour on, to paint your nails the deepest shade of red that you own, it is whispering, *he is coming and he looks like the last Christmas that you remember feeling happy*. Because when you turned 13 you started putting yourself in shoes that didn't fit you right, and kept going even though your toes ached and your heart felt like it was rubbing itself raw on the inside of your ribs. At 15 you slept with a boy who didn't call you and it hurt. At 17 you wondered if there was something about you that said you'd be lonely forever. At 19 you could barely look at yourself in the mirror without wincing. You will not know until it happens because it will not be different than any other day, because you are not listening to the sky, instead Half Moon Run is telling you to walk faster, and hitch your bag tighter on your shoulders, the evening wears you like an old dress. You do not know yet that when he comes he will touch you there, at the place where your schoolbags have been making ridges for years, he will hold you reverently and desperately because he has touched before but he was never this full of someone when it happened. There will be no fanfare and your father will not roll out the cavalry or cock his gun, even the flowers will smell the way they always have, even the streets will hold your walk the same. It will happen like this, your cheeks will be flushed from walking so hard, your chest will be a heaving mess, you can't remember the last time you went to the gym, you can't remember the last time you stopped running from your own reflection, you can't remember the last time you did not feel like your loneliness was suffocating the life out of you. The sky will be telling you to *turn around and see for once* but you're not listening because you don't know how, there will be no drums when you meet, your headphones will fall from your ears though, you'll pause to catch your breath and he'll catch up with you and he won't think you're the loveliest girl he's ever seen, he'll be holding the something important that you left behind, he will think you look messy and warm and flushed, months later he will put his mouth to the hollow of your throat and whisper, *I can't believe I didn't know what you would turn out to be.* But for now, he will give you your lost back, your hands will brush and all he will say is *hello*.

8

# FAIRY TALES DO NOT LOOK LIKE THIS

1. This is how it begins: in the dark, we are the very definition of 'fallen.' The night is draped around our shoulders. I have never loved you more than I do in this moment. I wonder if you can feel the throb beneath your claws. I wonder how it is possible that you cannot hear it.

2. It starts, as most things, like an accident. Boy, I found you bleeding on the side of a road, your thigh was split open to reveal highway lanes, you couldn't look at me without flinching, the first words you growled were, *fuck off.*

3. And I would have left you there except you looked so much like a wounded animal, so much like the wolf with the broken paw, the kind that bites before it realises that teeth do not hurt half so much when you are hopeless.

4. And you were so hopeless. We should have realised then that when we touched, there was ruin. Because there were stirrings on the other side of town, and our neighbour's tree uprooted itself from the pull, and they said it was the storm but really it was my breath on your shoulder–

5. Really, it was the way I tore myself open to fix you. Wrapped tourniquets around the bleed. Really it was the way that you looked at me for the first time, like you didn't know how to decide between snarling or pulling me closer.

6. They talked about how we drove each other to madness. How lovemaking and breaking plates began to sound the same. How every time we touched each other, something broke, inside of us or outside in the city. Boy, you began to drink whiskey like it was water. I smoked so many cigarettes you swore that when you kissed my mouth your lungs tasted of ash.

7. We learned how to grow around each other, twisted ourselves into vines. When you banged your knee against the table, I developed the bruise. My daddy shook his head and promised to shoot you, he did not know that your claws turned to butterflies when you held my face.

8.  You were falling apart before I met you. I did not attempt to fix the fracture, instead I sharpened your teeth at night, sometimes with a knife and sometimes with my tongue. There was always blood on my lips after.

9.  *Why did you stop to help me that day? — Baby, you looked too much like a crushed flower, like the world had stood on you, even your growls sounded like whimpers.*

10.  This is how it begins: in the dark, on the ground. I kiss your throat, and the entirely world shudders.

At the doctor's office this time—

you didn't ask my name but I know you recognise me because you scowl so wide that the entire ocean could fit in your mouth. We pause and stare at each other from across the room and the space between us stretches until it becomes elastic.

"Are you stalking me?" you sneer. The corner of your mouth curls up.

You're so small and thin I think I could fit you into the palm of my hands and keep you there, but there's so much vitriol vibrating beneath that body I think you'd bite me. Probably venomous. You look the type.

"Sod off," I mutter.

"Not so nice this time, huh?"

I smile sweetly, "This time it doesn't look like you're trying to choke up your lungs."

Before you can growl something in response the doctor calls you and you show me your middle finger before sauntering away.

## I CAN BE PATIENT WITH YOU

I can love you so gently it will feel like I am unpeeling you carefully from yourself. I'll take your clothes off and palm you shivering in my open hands. I'll stand with you in the light of the opening morning and will not be possessive about the way the sun touches you in places that I cannot. It's fine if you don't want to talk to me today, or tomorrow, the day after that is pushing it but I'll understand. It's fine if you pull back because you're scared or desperate and you think I'll be sharp. I'll be waiting for you right here and I won't be angry and it's because I love you. I won't be mad or sad or cruel because I love you. They say it's all desperation and lust from here on out. They say it's all teeth and nails but I've been there with you. I've left your body like a crime scene, I've left you red and plum with bruises and they're right. But everyone is too busy talking about the burn. I want to hear about the vulnerable too. I want to talk about the skin on your forehead and how it feels when you smile and I kiss it. How it creases and I think *he's happy because of me* and somehow that's lighter than anything I've felt before. I want to talk about the way you look at me in our quieter moments. Like I'm the most beautiful thing you've ever touched.

There's a street somewhere in this city that felt us love each other so desperately that it's crying from the loss. There's a car window that has my hand print pressed against it. God, I don't care if you're silent with me. I don't care if you're moody or terrified or lost. I'm going to go right ahead and love you crazily anyway.

## PAIRS

On June 23rd, my toothbrush fell in love
with the toilet seat and jumped over the edge
so they could be together
forever,
a suicide if you will,
of the inconvenient kind.

(I lived on mouthwash and chewing gum for two days
till I could find the exact same one
without all the emotional baggage.)

I guess what I'm trying to say is that
the spokes of my bike are useless without the chain
and once I tried to eat bread without butter
and it tasted like ashes.

If I am a cigarette, you are the lighter.

In all honesty, I don't work well
when we're not together
or when I'm between the lips
of someone who is not you.

The thing is that salt isn't right
without pepper
and candles need flames to work
and these silly metaphors
are the only ways that I can tell you

that I'm the toothbrush,
and you're the toilet seat
and together we're just right.

I'm having coffee on my own on a dark evening on the 5th, the sky looks like it's sweating off perspiration from a run, it's practically heaving. I'm listening to the kind of music that feels like it should be injected.

When you plonk yourself across the table from me I burn my tongue on my coffee.

"What the hell?" is all I can manage.

"I think you're stalking me," you say. You're smiling for the first time and it looks like the sky just before rain.

"I think you're the one who just sat his fat arse down and interrupted my peace."

You ignore this, "What are you listening to?"

"Right now? A really arrogant and obnoxious little man."

You smile again and my stomach turns and I soften for a second, until you reach out to pluck one of my earbuds from my ears and stick it in yours. Your ears are nice, I don't notice until I look at them and suddenly I don't know where to put my hands, "You better not have earwax," I warn.

You laugh and we sit like this in silence for hours. The spaces between us hum very quietly. Like a radiator that needs to be fixed. Like the breathing of a baby when it's lying naked on its mother.

# LESSONS

1.
Kiss boys whose mouths taste like plums and liquorice,
take, but do not give,
do not surrender to the urge to fall.

2.
Kiss girls who are silk beneath your hands,
swell around them until you become water logged, heaving.

3.
Leave forest fires alone,
do not look for smoke, when your body starts to burn
stay away from trees, get the hose.

4.
You are not an apology,
do not treat yourself like one,
your lips are perfect for kissing,
your hips do not spell 'sorry'.

5.
The roar of your voice is a lightning storm.
This is why the sky excites you,
because you were born from it.

6.
They'll tell you that you are ruined.
Don't listen. You are not an abandoned train station,
you are poetry in motion.

7.
There will be leaves in your hair from climbing trees
and falling from them,
sometimes it is good to hurtle.

8.
Loosen yourself into elastic
the next time someone touches you.
Remember: you are not an apology,
you belong solely to yourself.

# RUIN DOES NOT LOOK LIKE YOU

I've known girls like you.
Girls who are two shots
of whiskey straight,
and chain smoking,
thigh highs and red lipstick
and a mean old twisted mouth.

I've known girls like you at night,
you turn yourself into something new.
You're all soft inside,
you're all sadness and bite
and limpid, starless eyes,
calling random numbers in the dark
just so you can hear a new voice,
just so someone can say 'who's this?'
And finally you can breathe again
because you're a person again,
you're a who,
you're not a casual fuck in a bar,
not a wolf whistle
or a left behind, or an afterthought.

Baby, you're all heart and hands,
you're all deconstruction,
collapsed stomach and lungs,
scowling whilst you apologise for existing,
frowning as you look for warmth in bodies
that do not belong to you.

Wait, I want to tell you,
stop smudging your eyeliner,
stop turning yourself inside out.

Wait, I want to say,
your hips are more than a hotel,
wait for it—

your body is a place to stay.

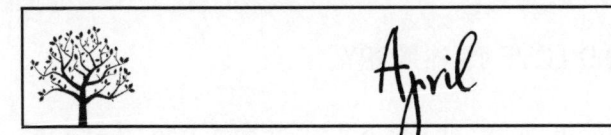

The first date you ask me to is at a broken down bowling alley, two streets from the train station. It smells of wet feet and deodorant.

There are teenage boys in dark clothes making rude hand gestures at me. I ignore them. You do not.

"Excuse me," you murmur in my ear. You look dark in a way I've never seen you before. My entire body trembles visibly when your hand briefly touches the small of my back and I nod. I am sure I would have nodded if you'd asked me to eat glass or whether I thought fairies existed.

When you come back, you are warm again and the teenage boys won't look at me.

"I can look after myself, you know," I say irritably.

You nod easily, "I know."

"Then why?"

You shrug, "You don't have to anymore." I turn bright red and change the subject by making a face at the surroundings.

"You're not impressing me so far," I inform you.

You tug my hair gently and wrap it twice around your middle finger. I pretend that my palms aren't sweating.

"You'll be impressed after I kick your ass at this," you say.

I beat you ten-two and it's only a little bit awkward.

## LOVE IS HERE AND LOVE IS HUNGRY

Mother, I am ravenous. Mother it is not what they said, they did not tell us the truth, they did not even say that it would look like the underbelly of a skinned mammal. That it would be like the inside of a lip. It is the scrape of his teeth on the soft of my arm and how I moaned for days. It is greedy and hungry. I am always hungry. I am always a stomach full of teeth and need. Need, god, I need. Once in the morning and once in the afternoon, sometimes in between. Sometimes I am not a girl, but a slice of desire. Mother, if desperation were human, she would wear my eyes. She would hold my hands. She would take me by the neck and fill me until I was boneless. Later she would write in her diary, *today I destroyed a girl and it tasted like wine.*

We've been swapping spit instead of stories. We've been trying to eat each other alive.

In the quiet moments, I have been picking cherry stems out of his teeth. I have been tying them up in knots and feeding them back to him. I have filled his stomach with pits. Every time, I have kissed it into his mouth and said, *I am a seed. When you tear me out, I want you to feel it in your throat. I want you to feel it everywhere.* I am wanting and longing, love is not what they said. It is not what we learned, or how we acted. It is full of tongue. It is full of plum. Grab what you need and keep taking. Gorge. Don't bury. Become limbs, become breaths, become the tiny spaces between your body. Inhabit, expand. Fuck. Fuck until you are raw. When you are both skeletons you will kiss each other full again. You will wrestle skin and ache.

It is not what I've read, mother. There is a monster inside of me. It's turned me into a body, it's turned me into nails. I am desperate for him. I am trembling for him. Love is furious, mother, it is so red and so ugly. At night we hold each other and shake from the violence of it.

## BLOOD LOVE

Here, we are savage.

Here, we are using nails instead of words.
Here, we are teeth and desperation.

There– bodies.
There is skin, no clothes,
we are beasts and we
are monsters.

Here, your name is more familiar than my own.
Your hands are choke chains.

I've loved you in so many places
I can't remember if home exists
or if it's a 2AM backdrop,
if it's winding the morning around our skin.

Here, you are breathing into my mouth.
Here, the air is coloured blue.
Here, the walls are sweating.

We've fucked in at least four different languages
but I can only remember one of them.

It's yours, not mine.

Here, we speak in groans
it's the only form of you
I know completely.

May

We kiss outside a Starbucks, under the awning. As always the weather does not adhere to the typical romantic comedy moments. It is not raining, there is a breeze so biting that I can't quite feel my nose.

I can feel it when you hold my face carefully between your hands, though. I can understand that I don't think people feel like this every single day.

I've never been held this way before. I tremble so much beneath you that I feel like a bird. You tap your fingers on my cheeks and murmur, "Nervous?"

"Please," my voice is shrill to my own ears, "I eat little boys like you for breakfast."

"Hopefully," your eyelashes lower and a blush stains your cheeks and I realise suddenly that you're shy too, "I'll be the last boy you kiss for a while."

Your mouth is as soft as I imagined, it tastes of the blackcurrant muffin we shared. I wonder what you can taste on mine. When we pull apart I think it's been forever and no time at all.

"Wow," you don't take your fingers from my face, instead you look at me like I'm something you've never seen before, "you taste like cake."

I roll my eyes, "you're so dumb, we split one remember?"

"I don't think I can remember anything I tasted before you."

"Fucking lame," I mutter, except it's hours later when I finally stop blushing.

# MY MOTHER'S LESSONS ON PEELING FRUIT AND KEEPING LOVERS

1. Hold everything very carefully unless it is your lover's back.
   Then, become metal, become teeth, do not gentle yourself
   for any man. Do not change for the ones who think that
   you should be softer, less mouth, less voice. You do not owe
   regrowth to anyone but yourself. When they begin to ask for
   you to shape yourself around them, leave. Shut the door
   firmly. Do not look back.

2. Do not waste what you have, use the skin. Lick the insides
   until there are seeds in your teeth. Share fruit with others,
   share fruit with your lover. Use your mouth and your tongue
   to discuss the inner anatomy of a melon. Remember that it is
   the sweetest on the 28th day, remember that when you open
   it, it will spill over your hands and his. Lap it up, after, bathe
   together. Later, you will find seeds between your thighs. Wash
   again, they lied about cherry trees growing in your stomach,
   but you never know.

   If the pulp is running down your arms, lick of the excess
   before it reaches your elbows. It's a bitch to get off, you will
   have to shower and you will find it everywhere– in your hair,
   and in all the lines within your palms. You'll taste sweet for
   days. He'll love it, don't you worry and if he doesn't? Try
   kiwis instead.

3. I've seen you hold things between your hands and crush them
   until they are leaking out of the spaces between your fingers.
   Learn when you need to be gentle, learn to caress instead of
   squeeze. If you tighten yourself around something that does
   not want to have you, it will destroy itself trying to escape. It
   will turn inside out. Do not force it, sigh and let it go. We're
   not talking about fruit anymore, I hope you know that.

4. There is a secret to the perfect cut and it is all in the holding of
   the fruit. Grip too tightly and you'll ruin it, not hard enough
   and it'll slip out of your fingers and your skin will learn the
   knife. Be careful with yourself, be careful with your hands and
   sharp objects. When you are eating avocado cut it through
   the middle, twist, pop out the seed. Do not attempt to eat the
   seed. This one tastes best in salad, try chicken.

6.  When you are holding mangoes be careful with the skin, take too much off and you're wasting the fruit, not enough and it's bitter to the tongue. Take it with you when you fall in love. Be careful with the skin. At dawn take him by the shoulders and lift him to you. Take his mouth and his hands. Undress him softly and then undress him further. When he is shaking in your hands, put your mouth to his ears and tell him that you will love him for as long as you think you can. If it is forever, simply smile. Nibble his ear. Let the light touch him with you.

# NOT SHAKING THE TREES

I couldn't tell you in any of the ways I knew how, it was strange because I spoke too often and so loud you often told me to shut up, but when I opened my mouth, I was always distracted. Your cheeks looked like freshly picked apples in the light. I wanted to sink my teeth into them. On Monday morning I felt the words rising in my throat like bile only I was stupid enough to look at you and I swear that I forgot what day it was because you were so beautiful standing in the light falling from the open kitchen windows that God himself couldn't have forced the sentiment from my mouth. And that's how it went, I tried and I lost it, there was always something to derail me and I could never explain to you how even the spread of freckles across your nose turned my stomach so heavily that I couldn't remember what languages I'd learned.

Sometimes I whispered them to you in Bengali at night whilst you were lying across my stomach, over and over again like the lyrics from a favourite song and you'd ask me in your sleepy voice what I meant and all I could say was 'I'm asking if you'll make me a sandwich.' You'd pinch my stomach and roll your eyes until your lashes fluttered against my skin and curse in frustration. Sometimes you kissed me so hard I wondered if you were trying to lick the words out of my mouth.

Just know that I tried to tell you in other ways, quietly and gently, I bought your favourite blend of chocolate milk and didn't let anyone drink it because when your stomach hurt you'd put your head on my shoulder and cradle the cup in your hands. I learned your favourite song on guitar and it took me three whole weeks to pluck up the courage to show you but I peeked under my lashes when I was playing and your smile, boy, it looked like rain on desert and it was worth the sore nails. You asked me to play on Saturday night, you told me that you wished I could say it, but I couldn't so I strummed it through my fingers instead and let you eat the last slice of cake. You must have known then, when I shook for you at night and held your hands until my nails were tattoos on your skin, when I sat through hours of Lord of the Rings for you, that even though you hadn't heard me say it yet, I was still telling you in a thousand different ways, I was still telling you.

# June

You hate horror films and I can't stand your pretentious indie movies so we settle on chick flicks and you laugh at every other word like a delighted and overly exuberant puppy.

When you're not laughing you're kissing the side of my face and distracting me, carefully pulling my hair through your fingers and trapping them between your nose and lips in a fake moustache.

"You're bloody annoying, you know that?" I mutter when you nibble at the corner of my jaw and I lose the dialogue on screen completely. This is no over-exaggeration; my eyes go blurry when you kiss me. My hands forget how to hold things.

When you surprise touch me I drop the things that I am holding. Glass bowls, mugs and plates have all been sacrificed because of you. I have given up trying to control all the ways that my body reacts to you when you are near.

"Do you know, right here," you murmur. Your lips are at my throat, "You smell just like lavender."

"Do you like it?" I ask against my better judgement.

"No, it makes me want to fucking hurl."

I punch you so hard that you complain about the bruise for two weeks straight.

# FEED

There's a feast in a dark room, only it's not a feast, it's a girl. But she's not a girl anymore. She's a body. She's a canvas and he is kissing her into art. She is art and he is using both of his hands to twist her into careful shapes around him. He is painting her teeth marks and raw and she is panting him into a new animal. There has been a fire here. There has been a hurricane. The floor is scorch marks and ash.

They are gasping air and fluid language into each other's mouths. She raises him and unpeels him from himself carefully. She raises him. Takes his thighs and his arms and his hips. Takes her own hips and introduces them. He whispers, *I'll take care of you.* Through gritted teeth. He can't remember his own name but he knows her. He writes it into her shoulder with his incisors. She says, *yes, please, god, please.* There is no god here. Only skin and thankfulness. Only desperation. Only sweat. There is no Satan either. The world is looking away, it is counting its fingers, and blushing red. It does not want to know or see that here, they are loving each other into dust. That they are nails and teeth and desperation. They are pressing body shaped holes into the mattress. The air is learning that there is another language in tongues. That it is heavier where it touches, that it tastes slightly like rust and se-men and is full of wanting. Here, she is pressing herself into him. Here, her mouth knows beg and plead. Here, her arms are the choke chains.

Somewhere there is a phone ringing, somewhere there are women playing rugby and someone has fallen down. Somewhere a fire is raging. Here, there is education. His hands learn intimately the cusp of her neck. The cusp of her gasp and shake and heave. And repeat. *Please god.* Lying on the edge of something so brutally gentle that he has to write a story on her breasts for her to understand. She will read it later. She will sigh and touch the bruise, and understand that he could not love her. Not because he did not want to but because there was an entire world standing in the way, holding up its arms saying, *you can be like this, but not for forever, not even close to forever.*

So they breathe in fits, in case their lungs get in the way, or their clothes get in the way or talking gets in the way. She tells him that she wants him by leaving a tally mark on his back. He tells her he knows but he does not tell her. Instead, when she gets home she will find that her mouth is sore. There, he has painted another story. There, she knows without knowing. They have ate each other into understanding. They have feasted themselves new.

Gorge quietly, the world is saying. Do not speak, groan if you must. Whatever you do, do not love, do not love. There has been an ocean here. There have been flowers in bloom. Whatever you do, do not sink, do not love.

# I AM SOMEHOW ALWAYS IN MID-SEARCH FOR YOU

I think you should stay.

The doctors said there's a gap between our hands that shouldn't be there. They said our fingers would continue to clench spontaneously because they are looking for something to hold onto. Don't start smoking, they told me, it won't replace the way that you hurt for him. They said that it would stop aching eventually but it would burn until then. They said you can't be homesick for another person.

I don't believe them though.

My legs don't like walking into rooms that you're not in. Last night I couldn't sleep in the bedroom because my knees wouldn't take me up the stairs. My thighs had told them they missed your hips. Nothing is agreeing with me.

I'm going to a cardiologist tomorrow just to make sure they didn't miss anything. Look, the thing is, I'm already on fire for you, I'm already leaving my doors unlocked and my windows open, I'm hoping you'll crawl back into bed with me, I'm hoping I'll wake up with your hands around my neck and your name in my mouth.

The doctors will call, I'm sure.

They're going to say, *there's a blockage, and it's leaking but it's nothing we've ever seen before.*

And I'll tell them, *yes, it's my arteries, they're tying themselves into knots, they miss him too.*

Your first asthma attack happens at 2am on Saturday the 8th. You shake so much that you make the entire bed tremble and I don't remember being as scared as that, even after all that happened between us.

We call the hospital and they take you away and put you on oxygen and tell me to, *go home young lady, he'll be just fine.*

Instead I sit on the floor outside the waiting room until a nurse gives me her hand and tells me that you've been asking for me.

It takes two hours for you to be okay again and when your lungs finally stop sounding like a tree being chopped down I climb on top of you and kiss your face all over, again and again.

"Gross," you say weakly. "You're getting snot all over me."

"I don't care," I press my mouth against your eyelids and purse my lips on your eyelashes. "You scared the shit out of me I love you."

Your hands are in my hair so fast that I don't have time to blink.

"Say that again," you demand.

"Say what?"

"You know what."

"No."

"Say that again or I'll have another attack just to spite you."

I elbow you in the ribs.

28

## THE WEIGHT OF LOVING

I am afraid that you are going to have to tell me, at every available
occasion that I am loved.

Because I am made of smoke and I will forget.

And my insecurities? I could fit them into the palm of my hand
but if I walked into a river carrying their weight, I know I'd drown
from it all.

And I can't promise anything but I can tell you that I'll never get
sick of hearing the words.

That your lips are a balm and I am so tired of keeping my head
from falling back onto every pillow I go near.

I know you can't understand because the nape of my neck looks
fragile to you and not heavy at all

but you can hold me with the glance of your gaze alone but I
cannot keep myself upright when I am alone or when I am lonely,

I droop like patchwork dolls and the nights you come home to find
me collapsed on rugged surfaces are the moments you love me the
hardest and the longest.

*Because you look broken*, you whisper into the shell of my ear, *and I
have to hold you together with the strength of my arms alone.*

I cannot count the times you have patiently set glue aside and
pieced me into the girl you know again paying special attention to
the size of my eyes and the sockets of my arms
because I gather you with those and you need that too, not always,
not as often and I'm sorry
that I dissolve so much.

Yes, I do forget sometimes when you are talking to me that you are
real and although I can't promise you much I can promise you this
I know I'll never get sick of the words,

so please, please, whisper them a thousand times over into the conch
of my ears, so I'll know, so they're the last thing I hear
before I leave again and the first thing
when I come back.

# IT IS THE END OF THE WORLD AND I AM WAITING FOR YOU HERE

<u>My hair is on fire</u>.
This is the third time I've extinguished it today.

I can't feel the tips of my fingers, but somehow I remember yours
they were everywhere once, I stopped wearing lipstick
because you'd smudge my mouth whenever you walked past.
I began to <u>look abstract</u>.

We spent our Saturdays with your thumb tucked between my teeth,
your hands between my thighs.

I'm as empty as church now.

I spent my weekends wondering if your legs are hurting,
if you are lying crushed somewhere on the side of a quiet road,
if the world has torn you into a new person.
When I think like this, I try to smoke,
only there's fire everywhere and it all turns to flame.

There are scorch marks on my thighs.
I wear short skirts and pretend that all the marks are your fingers.
They're not of course,
so I drink vodka straight from the bottle and ring your voicemail,
as the house crumbles.
I lie in bed and think of you.

Did you know that last night, the sky tore itself in two?

There was ash on my cereal, floating in the milk,
I ate it anyway and missed you all the while.

The last time we spoke you hung up on me.
I can't remember if you sounded hopeful.

There's nothing to look forward to much anymore.
There was an earthquake two weeks ago,
mostly everyone is gone now so the store is empty,
I don't pay for things anymore.

31

I can lie naked in the garden and watch as the world collapses.

The world is ending a day at a time
but I'm staying right here just in case
you come back to me.

Our first serious fight looks like the inside of a hurricane or a car crash. There is so much wreckage I wonder how either of us got out without broken bones. Something breaks somewhere inside of us, but it's not our limbs.

I tip all of your belongings onto the floor and you kick the wall.

"I hate you sometimes you know that?" I say quietly.

"Trust me the feeling is fucking mutual," you snap at me.

Your shoulder blades look like knives beneath your t-shirt, I want to touch you but my stomach feels like cement and I know that all you will do is shrug me off and hiss something venomous.

I try anyway to put my hands carefully on the small of your back but you flinch away from me so quickly there is open empty space where my fingers are. I hold the air carefully between my palms and pretend that my insides aren't aching from the loss.

For two hours we sit in silence not looking at each other. I'm afraid that if I do glance at you our eyes will meet and the apathy in yours will ruin me.

Eventually the quiet becomes too loud. I throw my hands up and try to stop my bottom lip from trembling and say, "Well, it's obvious that you don't want me here. I'll just get out of your sodding way, shall I?"

You don't chase after me, it's two days until we talk again and even then all you say is, "I left my iPod at your house can I get it?"

"Okay."

You don't look at me properly the whole time.

## SAMSON

God pointed you out to me,
rumbled, *destroy him,*
and the Earth cracked down the middle
at the sound of his voice
because I nodded,
I said, *yes sir,*
and did not count
for the way love would feel
against my chest,
not like any bird I knew
but the scissors I used
to cut your hair when you were splayed
between my open thighs,
golden, aching hero, you were
the most beautiful surrender
I ever saw,
I met your eyes in the mirror behind us
and fucked myself to that image
and cried every day for a year after
because even the bathroom mirror gasped
when I grasped fistfuls of your hair
and sheared it to the scalp.
You shook beneath me and it was like moving mountains
but you held the back of my neck still
and fed the words into my mouth
and they tasted like sin, baby you said,
*I am still strong because I am with you.*
*I am still strong because you are my woman.*
Our love was not what you thought
it was blood sacrifice,
it was war.
We spent two weeks lying in sweat and sex,
I kissed you until your mouth
was a bruise.
You couldn't lift cars from women anymore,
I wore your hair around my neck
and opened jars without your help
and whilst you were sleeping
on the holy Sunday, the sunlight cradled you
like a mother,

I crept in crying, and got salt all over your shirt
and you stirred like a baby,
pressed your face into my soft
and did not look surprised when the apostles came
to take you apart.
My toy soldier, I watched them shake you like a doll
and thought of how we'd loved each other
until our bones had turned to marrow
and even then, it wasn't enough.
Even then, I'd made a promise to God
and you swore he was not in that room with us
but he was, he was, and he was saying, *Delilah,*
*what have you done?*

## DELILAH

Delilah, they talk about forgiveness
as though it will come like a bird
with wings and save humanity
from itself.
As though it will arrive like the wave
that God has been holding in his palm
and cleanse us whole.
But I am not a man anymore,
I am not pure anymore,
if there is dark on my soul
I want it there.
If there is rust under my skin
I put it there,
as a reminder that I have commanded
these holy wars with the same blood stained hands
that I have had between your legs.
Delilah, I have seen death, and I have shook his hand
and told him, *I will not bow down for you today.*
But for you, woman.
Not goddess at all,
not immortal at all, not loyal at all.
I am splayed skin and bent knees.
I am blood and wine,
choking back a fistful of teeth
and eating at your thighs
as though your body is a banquet
and I have been starved.
Like honey and dates,
I loved you soft,
I loved you careful and
I bowed for you, Delilah
when my legs had given out beneath me
and the apostles were using chains instead of hands,
when their whips had turned me to ribbons,
I was on my knees for you
in a room full of Sunday sun.
I was cheek pressed against stomach
your hands grasping at my scalp,

they ripped you from my body,
and told you, *well done.*
And I knew that there is no God here.
I am not sure if there ever was.

At least you heard me.
I said, *give me your love,*
*or give me death,*
and you listened.

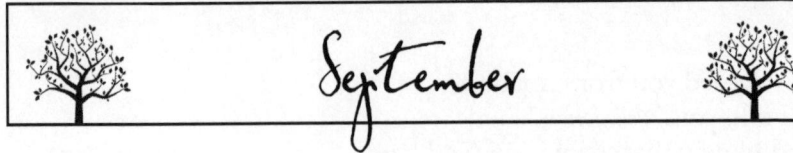
I wake up to a drunken phone call and you're crying so desperately that I can't hear you properly.

"I miss you so much. It's dumb but my asthma attacks are getting worse and I think it's 'cos my entire fuckin' body feels sad without you. The doctors don't have much of an explanation, they keep asking me if I smoke and I laugh because I think you'd kill me if I smoked, if the cancer didn't get to me first. You can't tell them you're heartbroken, or whatever. Does that even exist? I heard that the angel veins in your heart can snap from too much stress but this has nothing to do with my heart, it's all in my lungs. Maybe it's in my heart, too, I'm not sure of much anymore. I'm not saying this to make you feel sorry for me and call me back and let me say sorry properly, although I am a little bit but I really just, I wanted to hear your voice okay? Do you miss me too? Are you seeing someone? I don't think I could take it if you're seeing someone, unless you're like happy, I don't know, I just miss you and it hurts every day, I can't eat pizza anymore, okay. Who the hell stops liking pizza? It's the best food – oh god, I'm going to stop now. I'm hanging up. You've fucking ruined me."

# LETTERS FOR THE BOYS WHO BROKE MY HEART

1. First of all, fuck you, I am worth more than the £3.65 you spent on me in McDonalds, and the grimace on your face. I am worth more than the hand you brushed over my hips and the *are you sure you want to be eating junk food, babe?* I have stopped twisting my body into apologies for you, I have stopped interchanging water for food so you might find me sexy or pretty enough to fuck. Listen, I've forgotten what your voice sounds like. It turns out, I don't miss it very much at all.

2. I have always had a voice that is too loud to be a secret, and the first time you treated me like one, I went home and threw up and hated you for the rest of the night. We didn't talk about it after but you looked at other women whilst you were with me and I wanted to take you by the shoulders and ask why everything I'd given you wasn't enough. It turned out that it was, and you were just too stupid or too blind to see it. I don't cover up lovebites anymore, I don't pretend to not belong. I am here, I am here, I am here. Where are you?

3. I met you outside a convenience store at 2AM. You were pulling smoke from a joint and drinking beer, black leather and hair gel. When I walked past you leaned your hip against the cash machine and said, *hey baby, do you wanna come home with me?* I did, and I don't know why. I think I was lonely, I think I was looking for warmth anywhere I could find it and you were the first place I'd been in that felt alive. We stayed in your apartment for two days and only came out for food and water. The entire place smelled like sex and food. You didn't call me after. Somehow, I can't remember your name but I can't look at the brand of beer you like anymore. It only reminds me of how dark it feels to have someone fuck your body and not your mind.

4. There's a few streets I can't walk by anymore because my body is splayed across every inch of them. The roads here are wearing my teeth and my clothes and the way we loved each other. When I look hard enough, I think that even the cement is oozing the bite of us. I avoid the cracks, I try not to look at any windows. Your face is everywhere. Somewhere, in this city, there's a quiet abandoned apartment that has been mourning quietly ever since we left it.

Somewhere, in that apartment, is a letter I wrote you. It says, *I will think of you when the sky looks like it's trying to touch the ocean.*

5. On the first Saturday of every month I feel the ghost of your hands on my hips and drop whatever I am holding because the skin there is burning. Suddenly, I am all eyes and collapsed arms. Suddenly I am looking for something to hold. I have sacrificed mugs, bone china and all our porcelain for you. I am eating off of paper plates now. I have to drink beer out of cups. I am smoking more than I usually do because I know that you hate it. I'm hoping that somehow you'll feel that my lungs are still missing you and are trying to punish me for that. I think you were my worst addiction of all. They don't do anonymous meetings for lonely youths. If they did there'd be too much heart in one room, if they did, everyone would drown from the loss of it all.

# THAT OTHER WOMAN

That night when you come home
and drape yourself next to me,
like a cat that's found its place
you smell of Chanel No. 5,
not mine.

I want to scream, *how dare you*
*have the audacity to fuck someone*
*who can afford better perfume than I can.*

While you sleep, I lie in bed
and think of the ways
that I could hurt you.

Your jeans are hanging
on my drawer, you bought them
for £145, I spend the hours slowly
unstitching each seam.

When you ask I say, *God, baby,*
*I don't know, they scammed you maybe,*
*no one is trustworthy these days anyhow.*

For every time you put your mouth
on my neck I think of your lips on hers,
and the croissant I had for breakfast
rolls in my stomach.

I wonder if you know,
that I can smell sex on you,
I can smell longing for flesh
that isn't mine.

I think so hard that I get a migraine
and you say, *oh honey,*
*do you want a massage?*
In a voice I thought
was just for me but
no part of you looks

familiar anymore.

I look at your hands
on me, on her, on other hers,
your beautiful fingers
and I want to break them.

*You've been quiet lately*, you'll say,
rolling into our broken home,
traces of other woman all over your body.
Even when we shower together
I can't wipe the scent and I think
that maybe we can survive this,
except on our last night,
your hands are cupping my face
and you're saying, *god I love you,*
*you're the most beautiful girl I've ever seen.*

I imagine you saying those things to her
and I break like rubble,
the scratch on your face will be there
for weeks.

I'll show you the door, naked
and hurt and cold and I'll say,
*go to her.*

I'll say, *I know*
*what you've been doing.*

I'll say,
*I hope when you fuck her*
*you'll think of me,*
*you'll think of what*
*you lost.*

When you open your front door a week later, there is so much relief on your face that I don't know where to look first. Everything around you looks like grief.

You've lost weight, your t-shirt is inside out, your inhaler is in your hand and there is loud rock music blaring from inside.

"Can I come in?" I fidget as you stare at me like you can't believe I'm there, like I'm the best thing you've seen in a real long time.

"God, yes," you croak, rubbing your hand across your mouth. "A million times yes, please, come in."

"So you got really drunk, huh?" I ask. I fiddle with the straps of my jeans at my hips and your eyes fix on my fingers.

You smile sheepishly.

"Did you hook up?" I ask.

Your eyelashes flutter to my face. "Seriously you're asking me that? You're the only thing I've been able to think about for these past couple of months and you're asking me that?"

"Well?"

"Fuck no, have you?"

I can't look at you, "I really missed you."

"Can we try again, please, I swear I'll be better, I swear I won't hurt you, I swear I'll watch The Ring if that's what you want from me just tell me what you need and I'll do it?"

"The only thing I need you to do is start wearing clothes properly and take a goddamn shower, jeez, you stink."

# PLEASE LEAVE A MESSAGE AFTER THE TONE

Hey, I'm drunk, where are you? Are you okay? Is it cold where you are? You always forget your jacket, I hope you're wearing it, I hope you're always warm. It's so late, I miss you, nearly all the time, or a lot of the time. When I'm not sleeping I don't think I'm thinking of you, but I have dreams baby, I have dreams where I'm falling and someone is holding onto the back of my shirt, I think it might be you. I'd remember your fingers anywhere, I could hold hands with a thousand different women and I'd know which ones are yours with my eyes closed. They felt different somehow, like I'd taken a walk in rain and put my hands to a warm radiator straight after. That's what being with you was like, like being out of the rain.

I'm sorry I fucked it up so bad. I think that it's too late for me now, I know where your couch is. I know where you keep your condoms and the chocolate stash you don't tell your roommates about. I know the best place to get mobile reception is on top of your cupboard. I know that we both spent a Saturday curled up naked there together and it was so close but somehow it wasn't enough. It was never enough. Not even with your feet in my lap or your tongue on my mouth or my dick, I always wanted more of you I'm sorry I loved you into leaving.

The thing is, I fucked up, and at night I think about someone else sitting where we used to sit and finding out that the spot beneath your jaw makes you squirm and then I have to go running because I've never seen red like that. I've ran a lot since we broke up, my legs look amazing now, I wish you could feel them. It's the worst kind of possessive but I can't think about you with anyone else. Are you with someone else right now? Does he know that the backs of your knees are sensitive? Does he know that you eat noodles with your fingers? I hope he never finds out. It's selfish, and I'm sorry but I can't not mean it.

Look, can you call me back? Please, let's just talk. Let's go somewhere, let's get a coffee, I won't even try to wipe the cream off your mouth. I miss you, baby, I don't know where the best place to breathe is without you.

44

oh.
## ON IMPLEMENTING THE "JUST FRIEND" RULE

<u>Do not look at each other directly in the eyes</u>. You'll unravel like a roll of string. He'll have to carry the parts of you home. He'll have to say your name like it meant something. He'll have to admit that somewhere in the past he wanted to eat you alive.

When you accidentally brush hands under the table pretend that your entire body is not an ache. Do not roll your hips. Do not open your mouth. Sigh if you must, but not into his ear. Arch your back, groan, curve yourself into a question mark but when he gasps tell him you're only stretching. Tell him it doesn't mean anything.

When he reaches for you, back away. Tell him he doesn't have the right now.

This is what will happen. He will squeeze your thigh and apologise for it. He will call it an accident. Don't believe him. He knows what he's doing. Breathe through your mouth. Feel for his fingers later when you get home. Fuck yourself to the image. Head in between your legs. Bruises on your skin. Fingers on your body. Hiss his name.

If you look at him, he'll know this is what you're thinking about. He'll smirk and his eyes will darken into thunderstorms. Do not look at him.

Do not stare at the pulse of his jaw. Do not look at his mouth. <u>Do not think of the ways he softened</u> underneath your hands. Or the ways you met each other headlong somewhere in the middle. <u>Some place that looked like desperation. Smelled like longing. The air is heavy there. It's swollen from being caught on the edge of waiting. It's full of each other's names.</u>

Do not meet him hungry. Do not remember the times you loved him.

When he crosses his legs leave behind the image of you cradled between them. If he touches you pretend it does not hurt.

If you leave together, keep a two foot distance between your hands and his. If you touch in the dark you're done for.

If you touch him in the dark you'll lose yourself. He'll lose his reserve.

45

There'll be noises so animal that you'll go home wondering if you're really girl at all. Wonder if he's fire and you're storm. Wonder if two elemental things can exist at the same time without destroying each other.

Do not fuck him furiously against any bathroom wall. Do not groan his name into the curve of his stomach. Do not splay across his windshield like any divine offering.

Wonder if you can touch him without leaving yourself wide open. Wonder if you can look at each other without tasting sex and blood.

Do not look at your hands. Do not look at his. Do not think about the damage they can do together.

This is a month of being pressed against walls and kissed so thoroughly that I can't remember my name properly.

After, you ask me questions like, "What's 2 + 7?" When I can't answer you chuckle inside your throat and cup my cheeks and whisper, "I love you I love you I love you," over and over against the skin of my forehead.

"I swear," you say, "even when you're with me I miss you still."

"You know you're turning into a cliché right?" I ask.

You bite my shoulder and there's a mark for days and I smile every time I look at it.

## THAT GIRL

I want to be your late night phone call, and your drunken texts. I want to be your desperation. Your shaking and your hands and your whole heart put in my palms. I want your bitten nervous lips. Your jerk of the steering wheel when the phone rings. Your arm around the shoulder and hand around the neck. Yeah? Her? Yeah, that's my girl. Your proud and your stubborn chin. Your jealous kisses. Kiss until your body is full. Kiss until your hands are brimming. Kiss until you can tip yourself liquid at my feet. Full of heart, mouth full of promises and dirty wants. I want your shoes at the bottom of my bed and your toothbrush in my bathroom drawer. I want your morning breath and sleepy fists over sleepy eyes. I want your thighs. Your kitten naps. Your sullen and your grouchy. I want your fire. I want to be your zenith. Your first point of contact with the sky. Eyes full of sky, eyes full of sun. Your knees and downturned mouth. Your knees and your bowed head. Your knees and your knees and the floor and your goddamn knees. There is a mountain in Nepal, they say when the sun hits it, it is the most beautiful thing anyone could ever see. I want to be your morning sunrise peak. I want to be your mountain girl.

# THE FUTURE PROMISE

Listen, at about thirty we're going to be arguing about the floor of our one bedroom apartment. I want cream carpet and you want wood grain. I'm going to hiss, *we can't fucking afford it* and you're going to snarl, *we'll have to replace it every year because of that damn disgusting animal of yours.* After that I'm going to grab the cat and slam every door of the house and I won't talk to you for days properly until you kiss her nose and apologise for calling her disgusting.

You will kiss her nose because you love me, and then you will kiss mine and sigh and say, *I just wish we could have gotten a puppy.*

Just know that through all this, I'm going to continue adoring you. Even if you are a dog person.

It's not always going to be easy. At 25 I'll see you drinking with a woman from work and not understand that the arm you have around hers is to keep her standing straight because she's crying over a break up. I'll push you into the door when you get home and demand to know if you still want to be together. You'll rub your arms but you won't shove me back. Instead you'll just turn around and walk away. Later I'll cry because you'll be cold and angry and saying that actually you don't have to deal with my brand of crazy.

I'm sorry for not stopping to listen to you. I'm sorry that sometimes I jump to conclusions it's just because I'm wound around you so fully I think it'd hurt like losing a limb if I lost you.

We'll work like this though: I promise that I will pick up your snotty tissues when you are sick, I will kiss your mouth despite the germs, I will look after you.

The first time we have a proper argument over the way we want to raise our kids, I will storm out and you'll have to call my sister to find out if I'm okay. She'll tell you calmly that you need to back off for a bit and leave me alone and you'll spend your nights drinking whiskey wondering if I'm going to come back.

I'll tell you right now that I'm going to come back; I swear that I'll always come back.

I will wake you up at 5AM frightened because of a nightmare I had where you fell from a tree and your brain leaked out of your ear. When you woke up at the hospital you couldn't remember me. You will sleepy laugh and hold my hand tightly and say, *what am I doing up a tree? I'm scared of heights you big numpty.*

You will do this every time.

We'll work like this: I won't always have dinner on the table, but neither will you. We'll sit in our underwear and eat cold takeout and argue passionately over current politics. I will call you narrow minded and you will call me a feminist bitch. We'll kiss it out in the back garden naked from the soul outwards.

Ten years from now we'll be standing together in Ed's Easy Floors arguing over wood grain or cream carpet.

Ten years from now it will still always just be you.

We spend Christmas Eve on the bench outside of Co-Op. I'm wearing your gloves because I left mine at home and your hands are furrowed somewhere deep in my pockets. When they accidentally graze my breasts I yelp and look at you balefully.

"I'm freezing my fingers off for you," you say, "this is my reward."

"We met here you know?" I tell you.

"You don't need to remind me. I was just about begging for you to help me and you left me out in the cold, you stone-hearted cow."

My mouth drops open and I kick your shin, "You're awful, leave me alone."

You tug my bottom lip very carefully into your mouth, and our eyelashes briefly hold hands. For one second I think about how unfair it is that your boy lashes are longer than mine without mascara. Then I remember how they feel against my cheeks and you kiss that smile away.

"But if you die here I'm sure I'll be responsible somehow," you say.

You're grinning against my skin and I'm trying not to be a cliché but it feels less cold now, like, even winter can't touch us here. Like my ribs could rattle from the shake of it all but if you touched me, just once, there under the place my entire body beats for you, it would be warm all over again.

It's silly to say that as we sit on that bench outside the store not even holding hands, for once, the weather does what it's supposed to.

The sun creeps its way across the horizon, touches my cheeks and my hair like a gentle and jealous lover. You laugh and rub my shoulders and exclaim, "Look, the sun came out just for us."

Azra Tabassum is a 19 year old English Student and hopeless romantic who lives on the South Coast of England and spends her days crying over fictional men and cats that she does not own. She writes about all the love that has not happened to her and all the desire she has yet to experience. Her lifelong dream is to fall in love with a man with a beard and retire to a small cottage in Scotland to raise an army of felines, open a small bookshop and of course, spend her days writing books and eating chocolate.

54

# Gratitude

I have so many people to thank for the very fact that this book exists and is possibly on your shelf or in your hands, but the very first person that all my warmest thanks go to is Amanda Oaks. Amanda, thank you for believing in me, thank you for giving me this opportunity, thank you for seeing something in me that told you to give me this chance. I owe you so much, and I am eternally grateful.

Secondly, for the person who has supported me through this entire journey, my whining and complaints and self doubt: Caitlyn Siehl. I love you, you give me so much more warmth than I could possibly deserve and I'll spend the rest of our friendship trying to give it back to you.

And my wonderful friends, Ifrah, Emma and Grace, thank you for coming to my open mic nights, cheering me on and generally being wonderful. I'd probably be crying in a corner without y'all.

Everyone on Tumblr, you guys don't know what you've done for me, but trust me, it was nothing short of miraculous.

Lastly, my heart and my thanks and all my admiration go out to Mrs Watts and Mrs Hutchinson. It's been two years and I still tell everyone who listens that you guys were the best thing that ever happened to St. Annes school and the English department and me! If I can grow up to be half as wonderful, I'll be more than satisfied.

POEMS THAT INTEND TO BE SEEN

By Melissa May

## SPARKLEFAT
Poetry by Melissa May

| \$12 | 62 pages | 5.5" x 8.5" | softcover |

*SparkleFat* is a loud, unapologetic, intentional book of poetry about my body, about your body, about fat bodies and how they move through the world in every bit of their flash and spark and burst. Some of the poems are painful, some are raucous celebrations, some are reminders and love letters and quiet gifts back to the vessel that has traveled me so gracefully - some are a hymnal of yes, but all of them sparkle. All of them don't mind if you look – really. They built their own house of intention, and they draped that shit in lime green sequins. All of them intend to be seen. All of them have no more fucks to give about a world that wants them to be quiet.

"I didn't know how much I needed this book until I found myself, three pages in, ugly crying on the plane next to a concerned looking business man. This book is the most glorious, glittery pink permission slip. It made me want to go on a scavenger hunt for every speck of shame in my body and sing hot, sweaty R&B songs to it. There is no voice more authentic, generous and resounding than Melissa May. From her writing, to her performance, to her role in the community she delivers fierce integrity & staggering passion. From the first time I watched her nervously step to the mic, to the last time she crushed me in a slam, it is has been an honor to watch her astound the poetry slam world and inspire us all to be not just better writers but better people. We need her.

— **LAUREN ZUNIGA**
Author of *The Smell of Good Mud*

"*SparkleFat* is a firework display of un-shame. Melissa May's work celebrates all of the things we have been so long told deserved no streamers. This collection invites every fat body out to the dance and steams up the windows in the backseat of the car afterwards by kissing the spots we thought (or even hoped) no one noticed but are deserving of love just the same as our mouths."

— **RACHEL WILEY**
Author of the forthcoming *Fat Girl Finishing School*

Other titles available from
**WORDS DANCE PUBLISHING**

## WHAT WE BURIED
Poetry by Caitlyn Siehl

| \$12 | 64 pages | 5.5" x 8.5" | softcover |

ISBN: 978-0615985862

This book is a cemetery of truths buried alive. The light draws you in where you will find Caitlyn there digging. When you get close enough, she'll lean in & whisper, Baby, buried things will surface no matter what, get to them before they get to you first. Her unbounded love will propel you to pick up a shovel & help— even though the only thing you want to do is kiss her lips, kiss her hands, kiss every one of her stretch marks & the fire that is raging in pit of her stomach. She'll see your eyes made of devour & sadness, she'll hug you & say, Baby, if you eat me alive, I will cut my way out of your stomach. Don't let this be your funeral. Teach yourself to navigate the wound.

"It takes a true poet to write of love and desire in a way that manages to surprise and excite. Caitlyn Siehl does this in poem after poem and makes it seem effortless. Her work shines with a richness of language and basks in images that continue to delight and astound with multiple readings. What We Buried is a treasure from cover to cover."

— **WILLIAM TAYLOR JR.**
Author of *An Age of Monsters*

## LITERARY SEXTS

A Collection of Short & Sexy Love Poems
(Volume 1)

| $12 | 42 pages | 5.5" x 8.5" | softcover |

ISBN: 978-0615959726

Literary Sexts is a modern day anthology of short love poems with subtle erotic undertones edited by Amanda Oaks & Caitlyn Siehl. Hovering around 50 contributors & 124 poems, this book reads is like one long & very intense conversation between two lovers. It's absolutely breathtaking. These are poems that you would text to your lover. Poems that you would slip into a back pocket, suitcase, wallet or purse on the sly. Poems that you would write on slips of paper & stick under your crush's windshield wiper. Poems that you would write on a Post-it note & leave on the bathroom mirror.

HIT #1
ON AMAZON'S
HOT NEW
RELEASE LIST!

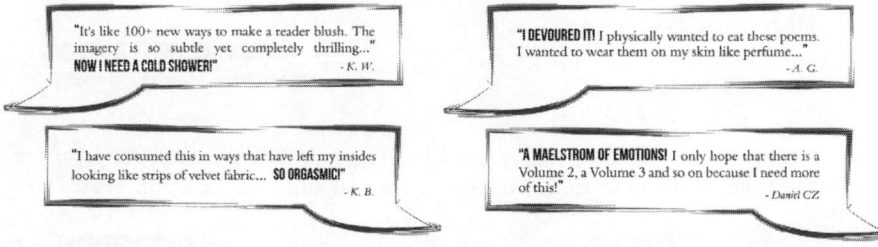

"It's like 100+ new ways to make a reader blush. The imagery is so subtle yet completely thrilling..." **NOW I NEED A COLD SHOWER!"**
- *K. W.*

**"I DEVOURED IT!** I physically wanted to eat these poems. I wanted to wear them on my skin like perfume..."
- *A. G.*

"I have consumed this in ways that have left my insides looking like strips of velvet fabric... **SO ORGASMIC!"**
- *K. B.*

**"A MAELSTROM OF EMOTIONS!** I only hope that there is a Volume 2, a Volume 3 and so on because I need more of this!"
- *Daniel CZ*

## LOVE AND OTHER SMALL WARS

Poetry by Donna-Marie Riley

| $12 | 76 pages | 5.5" x 8.5" | softcover |

ISBN: 978-0615931111

*Love and Other Small Wars* reminds us that when you come back from combat usually the most fatal of wounds are not visible. Riley's debut collection is an arsenal of deeply personal poems that embody an intensity that is truly impressive yet their hands are tender. She enlists you. She gives you camouflage & a pair of boots so you can stay the course through the minefield of her heart. You will track the lovely flow of her soft yet fierce voice through a jungle of powerful imagery on womanhood, relationships, family, grief, sexuality & love, amidst other matters. Battles with the heart aren't easily won but Riley hits every mark. You'll be relieved that you're on the same side. Much like war, you'll come back from this book changed.

"Riley's work is wise, intense, affecting, and uniquely crafted. This collection illuminates her ability to write with both a gentle hand and a bold spirit. She inspires her readers and creates an indelible need inside of them to consume more of her exceptional poetry. I could read *Love and Other Small Wars* all day long…and I did."

— **APRIL MICHELLE BRATTEN**
editor of *Up the Staircase Quarterly*

"Riley's poems are personal, lyrical and so vibrant they practically leap off the page, which also makes them terrifying at times. A beautiful debut."

— **BIANCA STEWART**

Tammy Foster Brewer is the type of poet who makes me wish I could write poetry instead of novels. From motherhood to love to work, Tammy's poems highlight the extraordinary in the ordinary and leave the reader wondering how he did not notice what was underneath all along. I first heard Tammy read 'The Problem is with Semantics' months ago, and it's stayed with me ever since. Now that I've read the entire collection, I only hope I can make room to keep every one of her poems in my heart and mind tomorrow and beyond.

— **NICOLE ROSS**, author

## NO GLASS ALLOWED
Poetry by Tammy Foster Brewer

$12 | 56 pages | 6" x 9" | softcover | ISBN: 978-0615870007

Brewer's collection is filled with uncanny details that readers will wear like the accessories of womanhood. Fishing the Chattahoochee, sideways trees, pollen on a car, white dresses and breast milk, and so much more -- all parts of a deeply intellectual pondering of what is often painful and human regarding the other halves of mothers and daughters, husbands and wives, lovers and lost lovers, children and parents.

— **NICHOLAS BELARDES**
author of *Songs of the Glue Machines*

Tammy deftly juxtaposes distinct imagery with stories that seem to collide in her brilliant poetic mind. Stories of transmissions and trees and the words we utter, or don't. Of floods and forgiveness, conversations and car lanes, bread and beginnings, awe and expectations, desire and leaps of faith that leave one breathless, and renewed.

"When I say I am a poet / I mean my house has many windows" has to be one of the best descriptions of what it's like to be a contemporary female poet who not only holds down a day job and raises a family, but whose mind and heart regularly file away fleeting images and ideas that might later be woven into something permanent, and perhaps even beautiful. This ability is not easily acquired. It takes effort, and time, and the type of determination only some writers, like Tammy, possess and are willing to actively exercise.

— **KAREN DEGROOT CARTER**
author of *One Sister's Song*

a poem by Kris ryan

Unrequited love? We've all been there.

Enter:

### WHAT TO DO AFTER SHE SAYS NO
by Kris Ryan.

This skillfully designed 10-part poem explores what it's like to ache for someone. This is the book you buy yourself or a friend when you are going through a breakup or a one-sided crush, it's the perfect balance between aha, humor & heartbreak.

## WHAT TO DO AFTER SHE SAYS NO
A Poem by Kris Ryan

$10 | 104 pages | 5" x 8" | softcover | ISBN: 978-0615870045

"*What to Do After She Says No* takes us from Shanghai to the interior of a refrigerator, but mostly dwells inside the injured human heart, exploring the aftermath of emotional betrayal. This poem is a compact blast of brutality, with such instructions as "Climb onto the roof and jump off. If you break your leg, you are awake. If you land without injury, pinch and twist at your arm until you wake up." Ryan's use of the imperative often leads us to a reality where pain is the only outcome, but this piece is not without tenderness, and certainly not without play, with sounds and images ricocheting off each other throughout. Anticipate the poetry you wish you knew about during your last bad breakup; this poem offers a first "foothold to climb out" from that universal experience."

— LISA MANGINI

"Reading Kris Ryan's *What To Do After She Says No* is like watching your heart pound outside of your chest. Both an unsettling visual experience and a hurricane of sadness and rebirth—this book demands more than just your attention, it takes a little bit of your soul, and in the end, makes everything feel whole again."

— JOHN DORSEY
author of *Tombstone Factory*

"*What to Do After She Says No* is exquisite. Truly, perfectly exquisite. It pulls you in on a familiar and wild ride of a heart blown open and a mind twisting in an effort to figure it all out. It's raw and vibrant...and in the same breath comforting. I want to crawl inside this book and live in a world where heartache is expressed so magnificently.

— JO ANNA ROTHMAN
MA, Coach & Conjurer of Electric Creative Wholeness

**WORDS DANCE PUBLISHING** has one aim:

To spread mind-blowing / heart-opening poetry.

Words Dance artfully & carefully wrangles words that were born to dance wildly in the heart-mind matrix. Rich, edgy, raw, emotionally-charged energy balled up & waiting to whip your eyes wild; we rally together words that were written to make your heart go boom right before they slay your mind. You dig?

Words Dance Publishing is an independent press out of Pennsylvania. We work closely & collaboratively with all of our writers to ensure that their words continue to breathe in a sound & stunning home. Most importantly though, we leave the windows in these homes unlocked so you, the reader, can crawl in & throw one fuck of a house party.

To learn more about our books, authors, events & Words Dance Poetry Magazine, visit:

**WORDSDANCE.COM**

Printed in Great Britain
by Amazon.co.uk, Ltd.,
Marston Gate.